Praise

This game-changer for corporate teams aiming to enhance their outreach. Edmonds Kozma's step-by-step approach ensures everyone is on the same page.
Tamara Nall | CEO & Founder, The Leading Niche

Edmonds Kozma's 20 years of experience are distilled into actionable steps that anyone can use. His success in the entertainment industry makes his advice invaluable.
Aaron Poynton | Author, *Think Like A Black Sheep*

This book explores the psychology of connection, offering a unique combination of scientific insights and practical applications. It's truly transformative.
Bryan Howard | CEO, Peoplyst

John Edmonds Kozma masterfully bridges cutting-edge digital strategies with timeless principles of human connection. *Finding A Perfect Audience* offers actionable insights on leveraging content to attract and engage the right audience authentically. This book is more than a guide—it's a blueprint for building meaningful relationships that can transform your business and personal life. Having this wisdom on your shelf feels like having a trusted mentor by your side.
Carl Grant III | Author, *How to Live the Abundant Life*

Finding A Perfect Audience gave me the tools to turn my passion into a sustainable business. Edmonds Kozma's voice is both encouraging and empowering.
Casel Burnett | Author, *No Regrets*

Are you interested in incorporating "Finding A Perfect Audience" into your business?

Explore John Edmonds Kozma's strategies and insights on his website at https://www.JohnEdmonds Kozma.com.

Scan here!

FINDING A PERFECT AUDIENCE

CRACKING THE SOCIAL MEDIA CODE

JOHN EDMONDS KOZMA

Leaders
Press

Leaders
Press

ISBN **978-1-63735-370-7** (pbk)
ISBN **978-1-63735-369-1** (ebook)

Library of Congress Control Number: 2025900096

Dedication

I want to express my gratitude to all the talented individuals who have worked with me over the years. They gave me opportunities to explore the use of social media in the entertainment industry, which enabled me to write this book.

Table of Contents

Foreword

John Edmonds Kozma is a beacon of innovation in an era of unprecedented digital transformation. During his career in the entertainment industry, which has spanned over two decades, Edmonds Kozma has not only witnessed the evolution of content creation, talent management, and live shows but has also been instrumental in steering them forward as the CEO and founder of Bang Productions. The company has become a leader in the new world of entertainment. But Edmonds Kozma's influence extends far beyond the traditional boundaries of entertainment.

Bang Productions is not just another media company; it is a powerhouse that has mastered the art of blending technology with creative storytelling. The company's ability to produce short- and long-form content, manage a diverse range of talents, and produce live shows with unparalleled precision has solidified its position as a powerhouse in the industry. Bang Productions is a Meta Media Partner and created a TikTok LIVE Creator Network Agency. The company reaches over 100 million viewers monthly, translating to 1.2 billion viewers annually. This reach is not merely a statistic but a testament to Edmonds Kozma's understanding of the intricate dynamics of social media and audience engagement.

In 2016, Edmonds Kozma revolutionized the comedy industry by leveraging social media. He signed Darren Knight, popularly known as "Southern Momma," and within just two years, took him from the trailer park to the Super Bowl of Comedy *Just for Laughs*. This achievement usually takes comedians 10 to 15 years to accomplish. The social media platforms gave him the tools to operate like a TV network. By leveraging this understanding, Edmonds Kozma propelled Darren Knight to unprecedented success and set a new standard for comedians. Darren became the fastest-rising comedian in American history. This was also the first time any comedy act achieved national success with social media. Consequently, his social media business model became the standard in the comedy industry.

John Edmonds Kozma is the host of the *Unimpressed Podcast*. He interviews individuals from various backgrounds to gain fresh insights about life from the foundation up. John's unique perspective, shaped by his belief in the interconnectedness of all people through the Quantum Field, helps eliminate bias in understanding life's structure. He is also the author of *Finding A Perfect Audience*, a book that details a system for businesses to cultivate an authentic audience. With his distinct personality and deep intellect, spirituality, and healing powers, many consider him a "Source Master." John's enthusiasm for innovation and exploration is evident in his continuous pursuit of new ideas and viewpoints. His collaborations with talented personalities such as Nick Cassavetes, Claudia Katz, Armin van Buuren, and Travis Pastrana have contributed to developing careers like Southern Momma and Ginger Billy.

Edmonds Kozma's book *Finding A Perfect Audience* highlights his profound intellectual depth and passion for discovery. In the book, he presents a universal approach to gaining influence on social media, highlighting the importance of using content to gather data and the crucial role of the law of attraction in attracting the perfect audience. Edmonds Kozma explains that the internet is based on the human nervous system, and understanding this connection can help businesses find their perfect audience, which traditionally takes a lifetime.

Finding A Perfect Audience is notable for Edmonds Kozma's ability to simplify complex concepts into practical strategies. The book outlines the process of identifying a perfect audience in three phases and offers detailed guidance for establishing or re-establishing a perfect audience based on demographics. It provides valuable insights for businesses.

Edmonds Kozma's personal life is as rich and varied as his professional endeavors. A graduate of Charleston Southern University with a major in Business Administration and a minor in Economics, his early life was marked by his passion for baseball. But beyond academic and athletic achievements, Edmonds Kozma's life took a significant turn when he experienced a spiritual awakening.

Discovering his lineage as a descendant of Cherokee Indians, Edmonds Kozma embraced his spiritual abilities, including clairsentience, clairvoyance, mediumship, and natural healing. This connection to his ancestry has profoundly influenced his worldview, adding depth to his professional life that few in his industry can claim.

Edmonds Kozma's spiritual journey is not just a personal story but an essential element of his approach to business. He believes in his ability to connect with the Quantum Field. These experiences highlight Edmonds Kozma's belief that life is a structure of interconnected experiences and lessons that, when understood, can be harnessed to create meaningful and impactful connections.

In Finding *A Perfect Audience*, Edmonds Kozma brings all these elements together. He shows how understanding the structure of life and the human psyche can lead to creating organic and resonant strategies. Edmonds Kozma argues that businesses can create harmonious connections that feel natural and impactful rather than intrusive. This approach, he insists, is not marketing—it is about creating meaningful interactions that resonate with the audience on a deep, emotional level.

This foreword is a celebration of John Edmonds Kozma's journey, achievements, insights, and vision for the future. It is a testament to his belief that human connection is at the heart of all successful businesses and that by understanding and embracing this connection, we can create content, strategies, and experiences that resonate on a profound level. *Finding A Perfect Audience* is more than a book; it is a guide to understanding the digital landscape through the lens of the human experience—a roadmap for businesses to navigate the complexities of the modern world and emerge victorious and deeply connected to their audience.

Marianna Kozma

Finding A Perfect Audience

"The book incorporates concepts from the "Quantum Field," known as the new realm of physics, and applies them to social media through content."

–John Edmonds Kozma

Introduction

Finding A Perfect Audience is a universal approach to establishing a position of influence on social media using content to collect data. Collecting data using content by the law of attraction to determine an audience is like learning how to live based on your experiences in life. The tone of the content influences the audience it attracts, and the law of attraction applies to social media because it stems from human behavior. Through my experiences in the entertainment business, I met multiple types of people, giving me different insights into their sensibilities and how they live their lives. When I understood the entertainment business model, I was able to reverse-engineer some processes within the industry and started using content, eliminating unconscious bias, which is the juggernaut of society. The internet is based on the human nervous system. Companies like Facebook, TikTok, LinkedIn, YouTube, Instagram, and Snapchat develop algorithms around human behavior that push their business agenda. While it takes a lifetime for a human to attract the perfect audience, social media creates an environment that expedites that process for your business. Grasping human behavior on social media enables businesses to manage their audience targeting effectively.

For industries, including entertainment, it is paramount to identify their paying customers. Rather than solely catering to the industry, the focus should shift to the audience. This approach must evolve to become more effective in identifying and creating the ideal customer or fan. The key to this transformation lies in understanding human behavior with content, a powerful tool that can equip businesses to pinpoint the best way to find their perfect audience. The data we receive from the content is the guiding light in our journey. When building a customer or fan following, it is essential to maintain the purity of the business's message.

The process is divided into three phases and consists of seven independent steps. Phase one is "How to find your audience," where we understand the business's *environment*, *foundation*, and *sensitivities*. Phase two is the "Execution of the communication," in which we learn the *tone* and *timing*. Phase three is understanding "How to respond to emotions" and then understanding the "Social media landscape or business consciousness on social media" of the business using content.

This book seeks to empower readers to overcome unconscious bias through content, allowing them to attract authentic customers or fans.

The demographics of the audience are crucial in helping us eliminate unconscious bias. They provide us with the information to build a solid foundation, keeping us grounded and providing a reality check against assumptions and stereotypes that may impact our business decisions. This process gathers data to determine demographics, enabling businesses to communicate flawlessly with the audience.

Businesses should utilize data to identify their authentic customers or fans. The traditional business approach could be more cohesive, as companies often outsource vital functions like training, marketing, and recruitment. Outsourced companies typically have limited knowledge of the business's inner workings. This lack of understanding can hinder effective communication and result in unnecessary costs. However, by leveraging data from social media platforms, businesses can access information that enhances their comprehension of their customers or fans, enabling more informed decisions and providing hope in these challenging times.

Life is, at its core, a structure—a series of interconnected experiences and lessons. Understanding this structure in business requires a profound exploration of the human psyche and the links between desires, needs, and actions. It involves mapping these connections to our strategies, creating a universal blueprint that resonates with the audience. From my perspective, this deep dive into the human condition enables us to craft an organic and resonant strategies.

Finding A Perfect Audience's approach integrates our strategies seamlessly into the audience's everyday life. It is about creating harmonious connections that feel natural and impactful rather than using intrusive tactics. We aim to make our message seamless in the audience's life rhythm. When we align our messages with the natural flow of life, the connections become meaningful, helping eliminate traditional sales models.

Demographics are the foundation of our decision-making process. They are derived from responses from customers or fans who are attracted by the tone of the content. In return, demographics show us market trends, consumer behaviors, and historical patterns. Instead of just numbers, demographics are a compass that directs all our strategic moves.

I reversed engineered how audiences are built today and how decision-making blends compassion and data. It is about sensitivities imbued with empathy, understanding, and a deep connection to the audience's needs and emotions.

Emotions are a critical factor in any engagement strategy. They hold great power and can sometimes override logic and reason. Understanding and effectively utilizing the audience's emotional responses is essential. The goal is to develop campaigns that resonate with people, evoke strong feelings, and elicit reactions beyond simple transactions.

When I reverse engineer how to build an audience, I realize it is akin to reverse engineering life because social media emulates human behavior. It is about starting with the end goal and understanding the emotional and psychological impact on the audience. I created strategies that achieve these objectives. This comprehensive approach looks at the broader picture of life and its intersections, and focusing on the audience is a precise art. It involves identifying our audience and understanding their desires, fears, and values. This approach ensures that our engagement strategy is customized to resonate with our target audience.

Social media platforms are not just communication channels; they provide valuable demographics. We can tap into this data using social media analytics to understand our audience better. These tools offer real-time insights into audience behavior, preferences, and patterns. We can better understand what appeals to our audience by analyzing likes, shares, comments, and other engagement metrics. Social media analytics also help us identify emerging trends, allowing us to stay ahead of the curve and align our strategies with our audience's changing preferences.

Social media is crucial in understanding and targeting specific audiences in today's digital age. Businesses must connect with their customers or fans based on their core sensitivity. Ask yourself: What is the focus of the business? The traditional model is about fifty years behind, considering the available technology. Now, it should be all about understanding the source of the business within based on its beginning.

Social media apps serve as a platform where personal and business interactions intersect, allowing for customization, testing, and real-time optimization of messages. Instead of solely being a broadcasting tool, social media also functions as a listening device and testing ground, fostering authentic connections. These platforms enable us to fine-tune our messages to guarantee their relevance and impact.

Creating the audience goes beyond a simple backward approach. It integrates life patterns with the audience's subtleties. This strategy respects the emotional core of our audience, uses data as a guiding star, and views social media as a crucial bridge. With this approach, our goal is not just to sell a product or service; we strive to create a narrative that aligns with the very pulse of life, ensuring that every interaction is meaningful and every message resonates deeply.

I frequently used words such as environment, foundation, sensitivities, tone, timing, emotions, landscape, or consciousness, and I often wondered why. I then realized the importance of *Finding A Perfect Audience*. All the stories in the world have already been fully explored, and most businesses need to understand directly from customers or fans to establish and operate their business on a solid foundation. We must progress by being innovative in the world's business sector. People must realize that with a large enough population sample on a social media app, data will dictate human behavior. In today's business environment, it is essential to understand who is financially supporting the business. We must develop and refine any initiatives involving human data by establishing a foundation with pure source data.

It is essential to recognize that social media mirrors human behavior, with the algorithm being the primary distinction between the two. An algorithm represents the platform's agenda, so it is crucial to understand the platform's tendencies to reach your target audience effectively and maintain balance within the system.

As I considered the question, "How do I do this?" I realized that the most effective forms of content with energy behind each piece produced are relatable, educational, and entertaining. Using these three types of content, we can attract a perfect audience that will connect with our offerings based on the *law of attraction*. This strategy provides a clear path and reassurance.

Audience

"Twenty-year resumes don't mean anything today unless you understand the sensitivities of your environment."
—John Edmonds Kozma

How to Find the Audience

The data gathered from content facilitates empathy, understanding, and sharing of another person's feelings when relatable, educational, or entertaining. You do not need to actively sell anything because customers or fans will naturally respond to whatever social media platform you use for your business. Empathy goes beyond recognizing what the audience needs or wants when attempting to find the perfect audience. It involves understanding the demographics that the data provides through the content. It is akin to placing a percentage of each demographic into a funnel that determines the outcome. This approach allows us to predetermine the answers for your business, akin to the "Quantum Field." We will be able to create a robotic-type audience that confronts you with the answers you need for your success.

Empathy enables us to see beyond people's apparent needs and wants, and data insights reveal the needs and desires of customers or fans. The demographic group with the highest percentage numbers would be considered the core demographic, so we must understand the reasons behind what they want. Why is a particular service vital to them? What emotional satisfaction are they looking for from a product? When we use demographic data to determine the creativity of the content, it resonates with our audience on a deeper level, addressing their emotions, needs, hopes, fears, and dreams. When the audience feels emotionally understood, trust is established, forming a lasting relationship between the audience and the business. Understanding and connecting with your audience starts with putting ourselves in their shoes—embracing empathy at its core.

Empathy goes beyond simply recognizing needs on the surface; it involves immersing ourselves in the real experiences of our audience so we can feel their struggles, triumphs, and aspirations as if they were our own. This deep emotional connection is the key to creating a bond beyond mere audience interaction. By understanding their underlying motivations and emotional needs, we can create content that strikes a deeper chord. This sincere communication addresses their apparent needs and their deepest hopes and fears. When the audience feels genuinely understood, it builds trust, establishing the foundation for enduring relationships between the audience and the business.

Understanding the Law of Attraction

"Science only uses two parts of the law of attraction to determine answers for humanity."

—John Edmonds Kozma

Integrating the law of attraction into our lives and businesses involves more than simply wishing for an outcome and expecting it to manifest magically. There is a tangible, scientific approach to how this law operates, which I have broken down into understandable segments after numerous conversations and reflections.

The law of attraction consists of three main components: the Law of Vibration (Environment), the Law of Attraction (Foundation), and the Law of Action (Sensitivities). Understanding and applying these elements is essential for effectively using the law of attraction in business.

- **Law of Vibration**
  This law is fundamental to the environment around us. Everything vibrates at specific frequencies, creating an atmosphere or *aura*. By aligning our business environments to emit vibrations that resonate with what we aim to attract, we set the stage for the attractions to manifest.

- **Law of Attraction**
  Many people are familiar with the central element that attracts attention: the nonconscious foundation of the business. *Feng Shui* emphasizes the nonconscious direction established at birth. This direction can enhance how we align ourselves to attract specific outcomes.

- **Law of Action**
  This involves instinctive or deliberate actions that support our established environment and foundation. It requires making specific progress toward our goals. It helps us understand the emotions and biases that may influence our decisions. It is similar to life's final glue that brings everything together, defining a business direction and comprehending all aspects that make it tick.

Practical Application in Business

Adhering to these laws in a business context means aligning our operations and strategies with the energies we wish to utilize. Understanding a business's origins can help arrange physical resources, spaces, and decision-making procedures effectively to achieve the desired results.

To achieve growth and success, a business must consider and balance three key elements: the vibrations of its environment, foundational direction based on origin, and actions based on demographics. The demographics predetermine the path to success. This approach leverages the law of attraction as a philosophical and practical tool.

P1 Step One: Environment

A business's **environment** encompasses various factors influencing its operations and success. These factors are then divided into internal and external environments. The internal environment includes employees, company culture, management, and internal processes. Creating a favorable internal environment can enhance productivity and employee satisfaction. Conversely, the external environment consists of factors outside the company, such as market trends, competition, economic conditions, and regulatory changes. Understanding and adapting to these external factors is crucial for strategic planning.

The term "environment" includes the current surroundings and conditions, comprising internal and external factors that impact a business. In this context, Facebook, TikTok, LinkedIn, YouTube, Instagram, and Snapchat are part of the technology environment. Social media platforms can be categorized into six types: social networking, social bookmarking, social news, media sharing, microblogging, and online forums. Each platform serves different purposes and user interests, making it essential to understand the tendencies of each app. Factors of the environment include employees, customers, supply and demand, management, government activities, technological innovation, social and market trends, and economic changes. These attributes shape the identity of a business in *Finding A Perfect Audience*.

Similarly, predetermined factors significantly influence our lives, affecting us even before our choices take effect. Feng Shui is often described as living in harmony with nature. Energy exists within our bodies and surroundings, and there is a constant ebb and flow of energy in our bodies and immediate physical environment. This is why having a wood-framed bed can affect you differently than a wrought-iron bed frame, as energy transfers from one object to another. Your physical environment can impact your body and intellect.

Now, how can we apply this knowledge to the technology environment of social media platforms? Social media platforms are akin to human behavior; we need to understand the dynamics and feel of each platform. When we experience success on these social media apps for a period, that success tends to decline eventually. We must recognize this pattern and tweak our approach to maintain success, understanding that the platform's algorithm aims to create balance based on its business agenda.

Many people are introduced to feng shui through the media. The concept of "chi flow" is often discussed, focusing on furniture arrangement, architectural features, and how they affect invisible air currents within our homes or workplaces. Several factors determine whether these energy flows are healthy or harmful.

How does this play a role in *Finding A Perfect Audience*? The company or individual must understand all factors within their technology and human environment. It is a remarkably similar process to Feng Shui. Take a moment to assess your current surroundings and determine how to enhance your success through social media based on environmental factors. All factors create a message defining how you communicate to the audience. A successful business identity requires a firm grasp of the environment. Learning about the importance of a company's or individual's environment is integral to improving success. Understanding the tendencies of your social media platform is crucial, as is optimizing your audience. The chosen platform is critical to *Finding A Perfect Audience*. Recognizing the behaviors of the social media platform used in this endeavor is essential. Given the current situation, we must consider optimizing the process to save time, resources, and money.

You need to document several factors, as they significantly affect your operations. Understanding the sources of the products or services generating revenue for your business is essential. Additionally, recognizing the top 20 percent of current demographics engaging with your content is crucial for effective communication with your audience. These demographics will provide a roadmap and insight to help you create high-energy, relatable, educational, and entertaining content for your target audience.

Gain a deep understanding of the numerous factors in your environment and then emphasize those elements in the content you produce. Start by sharing general content related to your business. When the audience interacts with the content, their feedback will assist you in identifying the demographics shaping the business's foundation and narrative.

Customer or fan reactions to the content will provide the data needed to start Finding A Perfect Audience. This information can be used internally to lower costs and gain insights into your business environment. When relying on third-party businesses for marketing, training, or advertising, it's crucial that they fully understand the sensitivities of your business based on the "environment" and "foundation." Without this understanding, costs can be high. A thorough knowledge of one's surroundings is essential for building a solid business foundation with data from social media.

P1 Step Two: Foundation

The **_foundation_** of a business is a critical element that determines its long-term viability and success. It encompasses several key components, including a clear vision and mission, a robust business plan, strong management, and an understanding of the target audience. At its core, the vision and mission provide direction and purpose, guiding decision-making and aligning the team toward common goals. A well-crafted business plan outlines the strategies for achieving these goals, operations, and financial projections. Economic management is essential for sustainability, involving budgeting, accounting, and investment planning. Equally important is understanding the target audience, which consists in researching customer needs, preferences, and behaviors to tailor products or services effectively. These elements create a solid foundation supporting growth, resilience, and adaptability in a dynamic business environment.

A "foundation" is the base upon which something is built. We will utilize the data from our content to identify our audience, which serves as the cornerstone of our business. Just as a company's or an individual's life begins at birth, shaping their identity and data (also known as demographics) creates the foundation of a business identity. Non-conscious thoughts and knowledge reside in a person's mind without awareness, much like a foundation. Collect the data from the content for 60 to 90 days (about 3 months) to identify the ideal audience demographics. This information is crucial for creating a communication strategy tailored to your audience. Based on my research, the top-ranked demographic is a 32-year-old woman with an annual income between $40,000 and $60,000. In online communities, women aged 25 to 34 are the most responsive demographic.

We must rely on data to establish or re-establish a business identity. The data provides answers to all questions about the identity of business. We can identify the perfect audience once a sizable group has been built. We can let the ideal audience emerge by eliminating the imperfect ones. We should focus on creating relatable, educational, and entertaining content while targeting the top 20 percent of demographics. Once we have identified this audience, we can creatively customize the content based on this target demographic. This content will resonate strongly with the audience because it originates from the core demographic, making it an authentic source.

Understanding your audience's demographics involves analyzing statistical data describing your core market's distinct characteristics and identities. This data includes their living conditions, education level, income, and lifestyle. Analyzing this information can provide valuable insights into your audience, allowing you to customize your communication strategies to better align with their needs and wants.

The concept of foundation is crucial in philosophy. It forms the solid basis for our beliefs, values, and actions. A solid foundation is necessary for the stability and longevity of physical structures, while a robust foundation is essential for a purposeful and satisfying life. This guiding principle shapes our perspective and gives us a sense of purpose and direction.

Why is the foundation critical in this case? The audience pays the bills, which comes first in any business. "Know Who's Paying" is a concept I thought of when I realized that big industries appeased their environment and forgot about who is paying the bills. The audience is the universal foundation of any business. Without a solid foundation, our ethical choices may lack consistency and can be influenced by situational factors, leading to moral relativism or inconsistency in our actions.

Demographics refers to information used to target a specific audience. The data obtained helps us understand various aspects of human behavior, which in turn assists us in developing our business communication. This data provides a framework for evaluating information critically, distinguishing fact from fiction, and forming a coherent understanding of the world. Understanding human behavior enables us to engage in meaningful and informed discussions, make sound decisions, and navigate the complexities of the information age with discernment.

Furthermore, establishing a solid foundation is crucial for the development and growth of a company or individual. It serves as the basis for building our identity, values, and beliefs, providing self-awareness and understanding of our strengths, weaknesses, and goals. This self-awareness enables us to nurture a positive self-concept, define a purpose, and make decisions aligned with our values and objectives. We become better prepared to handle identity crises, lack of direction, and internal conflicts.

P1 Step Three: Sensitivities

Understanding the **sensitivities** of your business is crucial for managing risks and ensuring long-term success. These sensitivities include several factors, such as market volatility, regulatory changes, competition, and customer preferences. Market volatility can impact your pricing strategies and profit margins. At the same time, regulatory changes might require adjustments in operations to remain compliant. Competition poses a constant challenge, necessitating innovation and customer engagement to maintain a competitive edge. Additionally, understanding customer preferences allows you to tailor products and services to meet their needs effectively. By identifying and addressing these sensitivities, businesses can develop robust strategies to mitigate risks and capitalize on opportunities, ensuring resilience and growth in a dynamic business environment.

The term "sensitivities" refers to understanding the needs and emotions of people and how they express themselves. This concept is like a casting call in the entertainment industry. *Finding A Perfect Audience* will identify the core audience demographics, providing information on communicating effectively within your business. The most important part of a business is knowing who is paying the bills. Social media platforms play a significant role in determining sensitivities in a company's or individual's identity. This model can replace a sensitivity analysis in today's business world because we can predetermine a perfect outcome. An accurate demographic is crucial for this purpose. Utilizing this data can gain insights needed to understand your business's sensitivities. These insights can be seen as "tools in the toolbox" that provide a clear roadmap for effectively engaging with your audience and setting the right tone for business communication.

Sensitivity analysis examines how changes in an independent variable impact a dependent variable under certain assumptions. Companies use sensitivity analysis to identify opportunities, manage risks, and communicate decisions to upper management. This practice often lacks value in today's tech-driven world. We can streamline success by creating content that resonates with your target audience. Doing so helps predetermine the answers needed for your business, allowing us to stay ahead with necessary decisions for the audience. When a sensitivity analysis is based on unreliable data, the resulting outcome can be off by 20-40 percent, leading to potentially costly mistakes in shaping a company's or individual's business strategy. Sensitivity is a fundamental human trait involving the ability to perceive and process environmental information. It consists of two essential components: first, the perception of sensory input from the environment, such as sound, smell, taste, and touch, and second, the cognitive processing of this perceived information, including deep thinking and reflection on experiences.

Understanding human sensitivities can help you comprehend how the law of attraction is utilized to cultivate the perfect audience. Social media mirrors human behavior, and the internet was designed based on the human nervous system. Therefore, I extracted demographics using content, creating a pure customer or fan source for a business. Each demographic provides the blueprint to understand the sensitivities needed based on the audience to align with the business. *Finding A Perfect Audience* shows how to mirror business sensitivities with customers or fans. The sensitivities of the perfect audience give detailed information on how the customer or fan reacts. This enables them to understand precisely how to communicate with their audience. The demographics help in defining the perfect audience.

The law of attraction is a philosophy suggesting that positive thoughts bring positive results into a person's life, while negative thoughts bring adverse outcomes. Simply put, a positive mindset will attract more success and happiness than a negative one. This "law" applies to all areas of life, including health, finances, and relationships. Recent empirical research has indicated that individuals who believe in the law of attraction often perceive more significant levels of success.

The last step of P1 is to set up the positioning, direction, and communications for the perfect audience. By understanding the environment, foundation, and sensitivities, we continue to improve our business.

P2 Step One: Tone

The **_tone_** of a business refers to the overall style and mood conveyed by its communications, both internally and externally. It encompasses the choice of language, level of formality, and emotional undertone used in written and verbal interactions. An effective business tone aligns with the company's brand identity and values, creating a consistent and authentic image. For instance, a company targeting young, tech-savvy consumers might adopt a casual, friendly tone with modern slang and informal language. In contrast, a financial institution may prefer a formal, professional tone that conveys trust and expertise. The right tone helps build rapport with the target audience, fosters trust, and enhances brand recognition. It is vital for businesses to carefully consider their tone to ensure it resonates with their audience and reflects the company's mission and culture.

"Tone" refers to a company's or individual's general character and attitude. Character is a business's essence and core identity. It makes the company or individual unique and defines its personality.

Understanding and defining the character is crucial; it is about introspection, asking, "Who are we as a brand?" and "What do we stand for?" This character becomes the anchor of all your communications, ensuring consistency and authenticity in every interaction. In the past, businesses built their audiences by assuming what customers or fans liked or disliked. Now, demographics from the content allow us to create the character of the company or individual without relying on assumptions.

The tone of your business is the attitude it conveys in the marketplace, combining confidence, approachability, and overall vibe. This attitude should reflect the company's or individual's character and resonate with your audience's expectations and aspirations. It is about striking the right balance between being authoritative yet approachable and professional yet personable.

Embracing this business core is the start of an innovative path of self-discovery. This path requires asking the profound question: "Who are we, as a brand, at our most fundamental level?" The tone anchors all communications, ensuring consistency and authenticity in every interaction.

In the world of consumer connection, people are naturally drawn to tones that mirror their own. This involves mirroring, where your communication tone needs to align with your audience's expectations and language. This synchronization is centered on empathy and understanding, communicating in a way your audience comprehends, appreciates, and trusts.

Like any aspect of your brand, tone is not static. It needs continuous evolution and improvement, which involves listening to feedback, understanding audience shifts, and adapting accordingly. It is about staying relevant, resonating with changing audience dynamics, and ensuring that your tone always aligns with your brand's evolving character.

How does this relate to *Finding A Perfect Audience*? The data from the content gives you these answers in one place. It is a road map for establishing or re-establishing an audience for a business. Adapting your tone to match their values and communication style is essential. Your tone goes beyond just speaking; it reflects the heart and soul of your brand. Mastering the tone is a branding exercise and a journey toward creating a robust and lasting connection with your audience.

A brand's essence, painstakingly crafted through its tone, slices through the chaos of the audience, much like a sincere smile mirrors the human spirit. This fundamental core, a testament to profound understanding and unwavering resolve, sets you apart from the sea of competitors. This captivating essence compels people to acknowledge and connect with you, transforming them from fleeting customers into steadfast companions on your brand's voyage.

The environment, foundation, and sensitivities used to develop P1 of *Finding A Perfect Audience* will set the tone for communication and evolve as the content improves. Based on the law of attraction, a confident tone will attract a similar audience. It is about striking the right balance between the business's voice and the audience's language.

P2 Step Two: Timing

The **timing** of a business significantly impacts its success, as it involves launching products or services at the most opportune moment. Understanding market trends, consumer behavior, and economic conditions is crucial for timing. For instance, entering a market during a period of high demand or when a gap is identified can lead to rapid growth and profitability. Additionally, aligning the launch with seasonal trends or events can maximize visibility and sales. However, launching too early or too late can result in missing potential market share or facing intense competition. Therefore, conducting thorough market research and remaining adaptable to changes can help entrepreneurs decide when to introduce their business to the market.

"Timing" influences how a target audience responds to messages. Communicators must deliver messages to decision-makers when they are most open to receiving them, considering the overwhelming amount of information from multiple sources and channels.

Understanding the importance of timing involves coordinating with your audience's market needs. It means being aware of subtle mood changes, varying interest levels, and shifting public sentiment. The audience's demographics will determine when they want to be contacted, so it is crucial to understand the tendencies of different demographics and social media platforms. This awareness enables us to make our moves in a manner that best connects with our audience, ensuring maximum impact and engagement.

Timing various activities requires careful consideration of when to launch a product, start a promotional campaign, and make critical announcements. These decisions are not made arbitrarily but result from thorough planning and analysis. The behavior patterns of the perfect audience will be determined based on their demographic percentages.

In the realm of perfect timing, asking the right questions is essential. These questions include: "What is the best time to reach our audience?" "When are they most receptive?" and "How do our timing decisions align with our overall strategy?" The answers form the cornerstone of our timing strategy, ensuring that every action is well-planned and well-timed. Understanding the demographics of our ideal audience helps eliminate many previously necessary processes.

Timing involves synchronizing our strategies with the market's rhythm and the audience's heartbeat. It is about striking the right balance between action and patience, knowing when to seize the moment and when to wait for the perfect opportunity. Mastering timing is not just about strategic planning; it requires cultivating an intuitive understanding of the ideal moment to act.

Interactive Timing Exercises

The interactive exercises below are designed to help you analyze your business timing decisions. These exercises will refine your instincts and improve your ability to determine the perfect timing for different business activities. In consumer connectionism and business, timing is not just a concept but an art.

Exercise 1: Reflective Analysis of Past Campaigns

The first exercise takes you on a reflective journey through your past promotional campaigns.

Task: Select three past promotional initiatives. For each, write down when it was launched, its duration, and its impact.

Objective: To analyze and understand the *when* and *why* behind the success or failure of these campaigns. Did the timing align with noteworthy events, seasons, or audience availability?

Outcome: This exercise aims to understand how timing influences the results of these initiatives.

Exercise 2: The Timing Mind Map

This exercise involves creating a mind map that connects your business activities with various timing elements.

Task: Create a mind map linking different business activities (like product launches, sales, or promotional campaigns) with timing elements (such as seasons, holidays, economic cycles, or significant events). This mind map will become your business's timing guide. Consider seasons, holidays, economic trends, and even substantial events—anything that could influence your plan.

Objective: To visually represent how different timing elements impact various business activities.

Outcome: This exercise enhances your ability to foresee and plan how external timing factors can influence your business decisions.

Exercise 3: Feedback Loop Implementation

The final exercise establishes a feedback loop to improve timing decisions continuously.

Task: Create a system for collecting and analyzing feedback on the timing of your business activities.

Objective: Establish a mechanism for ongoing learning and improvement in timing decisions.

Outcome: This exercise is more than just providing one-time insights; it is about creating a dynamic approach to timing across the company. Understanding your audience's dynamic needs and wants allows you to learn and constantly change your content approach. This mobility lets you reach consumers optimally, increasing engagement and keeping your brand at the top of their minds.

These interactive exercises are designed not just as tasks but as transformative steps toward mastering the art of timing in business. By engaging with them, you will develop a more nuanced understanding and instinct for timing, enabling you to make decisions that are not only strategically sound but also perfectly timed.

P3 Step One: Emotions

The **emotions** of your business reflect its culture, values, and the experiences it creates for employees and customers. A business imbued with positive emotions such as passion, enthusiasm, and empathy can foster a vibrant workplace atmosphere that motivates employees and enhances productivity. Customer interactions often mirror this emotional engagement, increasing satisfaction and loyalty. Conversely, a business environment characterized by stress, indifference, or negativity can lead to high turnover and a decline in customer trust. Businesses can create a positive emotional foundation that drives sustained success and growth by prioritizing emotional intelligence and cultivating a supportive and inclusive atmosphere.

"Emotions" are a natural, intuitive state of mind. Establishing P1 and P2 and developing the *Finding A Perfect Audience* concept provide a business with the necessary balance to handle audience emotions effectively. Managing emotions in businesses sometimes leads to impulsive decisions. Now that we have established a foundation and understand how to convey our message correctly, we can analyze the audience's emotional reactions to make minor improvements without completely disrupting or changing the direction of the business. Creating consistency in *Finding A Perfect Audience* helps us worry less about the algorithm.

The social media algorithm consists of rules, signals, and data that determine how content is ranked, filtered, and recommended to users on social media platforms. It aims to enhance user experience by making feeds exciting and engaging. The algorithm organizes content based on how likely each user likes and interacts with it. It fosters balance and supports the social media app's business model. Suppose your content is successful for a certain period, and we start to see a decline in that success. In that case, it must be updated or replaced to maintain sustainability according to the concept of *Finding A Perfect Audience*.

Emotions are a crucial factor in decision-making for consumer behavior and organizational strategies. However, they are often undervalued in strategic planning. They can influence perceptions, choices, and activities, from product development to engagement strategies. Understanding the impact of emotions on decision-making allows companies and individuals to create more effective initiatives, consumer-centric products, and positive customer experiences. By considering their target audience's emotional needs and desires, organizations can develop messaging and products that resonate deeply with their customers. Additionally, strategically leveraging emotions can motivate employees and improve productivity. For instance, fostering a positive and supportive work environment can increase employee engagement and productivity.

Understanding your audience's emotions goes beyond recognizing their initial reactions; it involves comprehending their deeper inclinations and predispositions. Since social media is crafted based on human behavior, the data we collect assists us in understanding this information. Aligning your business strategy with these emotional currents ensures that your message resonates on a deeper, more personal level.

Connecting emotionally to build and maintain trust with your audience is necessary. Maintaining a consistent emotional tone in your communication and brand presence creates a stable and predictable emotional environment that your audience can rely on. This strategy fosters loyalty and strengthens the connection with your brand.

Emotions are essential in business strategy. Mastering emotions goes beyond understanding how they impact decision-making; it involves integrating this understanding into every aspect of your business. This includes communicating value to customer service, product design, and company culture.

Emotions are the feelings we experience in response to events and situations. They encompass happiness, sadness, anger, fear, surprise, and disgust. When we experience emotions, our body responds with changes such as a faster heartbeat or tense muscles. These feelings can also manifest in our behavior, such as smiling when we are happy or frowning when we are upset.

Emotions help us navigate situations, communicate with others, and make decisions. They are a natural part of being human. Understanding our environment, foundation, and sensitivities allows us to anticipate emotions on our journey through life while finding a perfect audience. We eliminate the wrong customers or fans and obtain the insights we need from demographics that help us understand the emotions projected by the business. The projected emotions will assist us in making micro-improvements while running a fluid business.

P3 Step Two:
Social Media Landscape

In today's digital age, the ***social media landscape*** for businesses is vital to their overall strategy. It is a dynamic platform for engaging with a diverse audience, building brand awareness, and fostering customer loyalty. Businesses leverage popular platforms like Facebook, Instagram, Twitter, TikTok, Snapchat, YouTube, and LinkedIn to share content that resonates with their target audience, including promotional materials and interactive posts encouraging community participation. Analytics tools within these platforms provide valuable insights into user behavior, enabling businesses to tailor their strategies for maximum impact. Additionally, social media is an effective channel for customer service, allowing for real-time interaction and feedback. By maintaining a consistent and authentic presence across these platforms, businesses can enhance their visibility, drive website traffic, and boost their bottom line.

The "social media landscape" encompasses all social media platforms in the digital world. Choosing the right platform for establishing or re-establishing a business's audience is crucial in *Finding A Perfect Audience*. Once we have gathered and analyzed data, we gain insights into operating the business effectively. It is like a life experience. Once we have lived and learned, we understand what works and what does not work for us. We continue to perfect the process without wavering because we know our environment. We have established a strong foundation based on the data we collected and learned how to use our sensitivities to convey the business's message correctly. These sensitivities reflect the tone we relate to our audience, as tone attracts like tone. Our audience naturally developed due to human behavior and the law of attraction. We can communicate at the appropriate times based on the audience's demographics, which inform us when to send a message. We understand how to manage emotional responses to implement micro improvements for the business. At this point, we have navigated the social media landscape for the business, as we have created a perfect audience.

Our mood and persona are like a landscape, constantly adjusting and transforming. As we move beyond our experiences, some of our old behaviors may disappear. This concept aligns with life because social media mirrors human behavior.

The *business landscape* refers to the environment in which a business operates. It is influenced by various internal and external factors that impact its strategies, operations, and potential for success. The demographics can determine this because it tells us who is paying the bills, helping us eliminate traditional models that have been ineffective for many years. Businesses must know who pays the bills and not get into a pattern of appeasing their environment, forgetting about societal changes. *Finding A Perfect Audience* concept can save businesses 30–40 percent of operating costs. We eliminate the wrong customers, save time, and create the perfect audience to streamline the business.

Why AI Software Needs "Finding A Perfect Audience"?

Artificial intelligence (AI) is a branch of computer science that enables machines to perform tasks that typically necessitate human intelligence. AI systems can learn from experience, enhance performance, and operate with minimal human oversight. They can also perform functions that demand human-like perception, planning, cognition, communication, and physical action.

AI utilizes algorithms, data, and computational power to simulate human intelligence. This enables machines to:

- **Understand language:** AI systems can comprehend, interpret, and generate human language.
- **Learn:** AI systems can learn and improve from experience without explicit programming.
- **Recognize patterns:** AI systems can identify patterns.
- **Solve problems:** AI systems can solve problems.
- **Make decisions:** AI systems can make predictions, recommendations, or decisions that impact real or virtual environments.

The rapid development of artificial intelligence has a profound impact on every industry, shaping the future of humanity. AI is driving the emergence of transformative technologies like big data, robotics, and the Internet of Things (IoT). In addition, generative AI has expanded its reach and appeal. It is important to note that the excitement of innovative technology may blind you to potential issues.

The AI revolution is well underway, but it may not be as flawless as developers claim. AI excels at mathematical and architectural tasks, providing quick and accurate answers. Even AI that designs digital art is getting close to being correct, but the spelling and design need work. However, when human behavior is involved, the data it relies on must be sourced from reliable information.

While AI can speed up the process of obtaining answers driven by human behavior, the quality of the results remains the same. Until corporations start using *Finding A Perfect Audience* to establish or re-establish their audience, removing undesirable customers or fans and creating a perfect audience base, they will continue to make costly mistakes by relying on AI-driven human data for answers. Most businesses do not know who their actual customer or fan is because of incomplete data and lazy business practices. *Finding A Perfect Audience,* if appropriately implemented, corporations can save about 30–40 percent on the bottom line. It is not a quick fix and takes much work, but it can bring your business tenfold success in the long run. AI's full capabilities will not be realized as soon as we think.

Conclusion

As we wrap up *Finding A Perfect Audience,* our comprehensive exploration of consumer connection, audience engagement, and the digital landscape, it is evident that our journey is not simply ending but rather reasserting our understanding. This journey has allowed us to delve deeper into the essence of successful businesses using human connection. Beyond mere business transactions, organizations must establish genuine emotional bonds with their customers or fans. This necessitates a thorough understanding of audience psychology and the ability to create narratives that resonate with individuals personally. Additionally, infusing empathy into every customer journey stage is vital for cultivating long-term loyalty and advocacy. Businesses can discover new opportunities for growth, innovation, and societal impact by prioritizing human connection as a cornerstone of their business strategy.

At the heart of our strategy lies the power of human connection. From understanding the environment, foundation, and sensitivities of our business in P1 to mastering the nuances of timing and tone in P2 and navigating the ever-evolving emotional responses and social media landscape in P3, the end goal is to form a meaningful relationship with our audience. It is about looking beyond transactions and regard every customer or fan as a part of our extended business family—a relationship based on trust, understanding, and mutual growth.

Furthermore, prioritizing a human-centric approach enhances brand loyalty and advocacy. By emphasizing emotional connections, we empower our consumers to become passionate brand ambassadors, thus extending our influence through word-of-mouth recommendations. By investing in meaningful connections, we equip ourselves to address challenges and seize opportunities with increased resilience and adaptability. Establishing a solid foundation of trust and understanding enables us to navigate challenging times and take advantage of emerging trends, ensuring long-term success and sustainability.

It is crucial to uphold our values, adapt our strategies, and prioritize the human element in all our business activities. Authenticity and sincerity are our greatest assets in achieving success. Continuous learning is essential for success in both business and life. Having a clear sense of purpose is crucial. Our organization aims to increase employee and customer engagement by aligning our goals with a larger mission. Success should not be measured solely by financial indicators but by our positive impact on stakeholders and the world.

The *Finding A Perfect Audience* concept will redefine business strategy and audience empathy, showing customers or fans a fresh perspective and a clear direction. These strategies and insights are not simply about achieving business success; they also highlight the significance of human connection in the business world. Today, we step into the future confidently, equipped with the knowledge that our success lies in the harmonious blend of strategy and human empathy.